49 Excuses for Not Doing Your Homework

Copyright © 2014, 2022 by James Warwood

Published by Curious Squirrel Press

All rights reserved

No part of this book may be used, stored or reproduced in any manner whatsoever without written permission from the author or publisher.

Book cover design by: James Warwood
Book interior design by: Mala Letra / Lic. Sara F. Salomon

ISBN: 9798423774318
ebook ISBN: B0006APZ7I

# THE EXCUSE ENCYCLOPEDIA

Book Three:
49 Excuses for Not Doing Your Homework

James Warwood

## BOOK THREE

### Excuses for Not Doing Your Homework

# HOMEWORK EXCUSES

# 1. THE MIX-UP EXCUSE

What? You're collecting *Maths* homework this morning? But I did the *Reading* homework . . .

. . . Oh I know what's happened. I've accidentally mixed-up my maths homework with my little sisters homework to read *'The Hungry Caterpillar'*. I hope little Suzie didn't struggle with those algebraic equations.

# 2. THE NEWLY QUALIFIED EXCUSE

I signed up to a *'Fast Track Teacher Training Course'* over the weekend . . .

. . . my Teaching Certificate, accredited by *UniversityForDummies.com,* came through the post this morning and I got a Distinction! So if you'd care to take a seat I'll take it from here Miss.

# 3. THE NASA EXCUSE

My application to the 'NASA Young Astronauts Program' has come back. I've been accepted . . .

. . . From now on my homework is set by the NASA Officials. My homework this week is to: eat a mars bar everyday, practice my zero gravity walk, and learn how to countdown from 10 in a deep and dramatic voice.

# 4. THE ALIEN SPA EXCUSE

You'll never guess what happened to me last night . . .

. . . I was abducted by Aliens! They took me to their Spa Therapy Spaceship and gave me an *'Intergalactic Mud Bath'*, *'Slug Slime Facial'*, and an *'Asteroid Field Massage'*. It was so cool that I signed you up as their next applicant. Hope you have a relaxing evening Miss.

# 5. THE HAMSTER-NAPPED EXCUSE

I was about to do my homework last night, when I found this Ransom Note in my Maths Book...

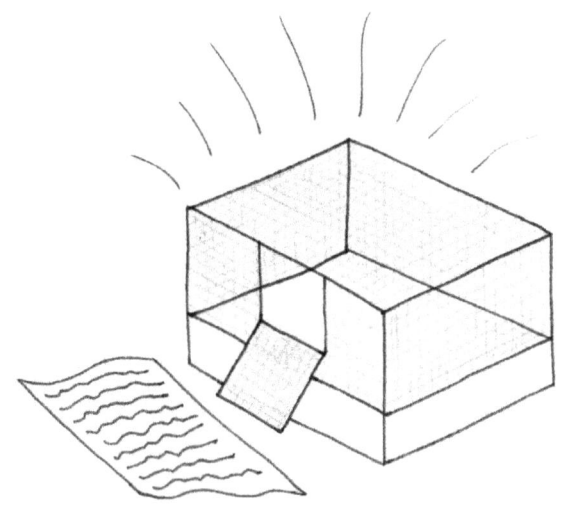

... Someone's hamster-napped Hammy the Class Hamster! They want all our dinner money and absolutely no homework for a whole week. I think you'll agree it's our only option!

49 Excuses for Not Doing Your Homework

# 6. THE GENIUS EXCUSE

Did you hear about the kid who has a higher IQ than Albert Einstein? . . .

. . . That's me. I'll be setting all the homework from now on, and try to keep up Miss.

# 7. THE BAD HEARING EXCUSE

Oh no! I must have misheard you . . .

. . . I thought you said 'don't forget your English home *jerk*'. I drew this picture of William Shakespeare with goofy glasses because Macbeth goes on for far too long without any cool explosions or car chases!

# 8. THE COPYRIGHT EXCUSE

Big news everyone. I've bought the copyright to the word *'Homework'*...

... From now on no-one is allowed to say, write, print, or even whisper *MY WORD* without my prior permission. You were saying Miss... something about me forgetting to do something?

# 9. THE HEAD-START EXCUSE

I got bored of all the *easy* homework you've been setting lately . . .

. . . So I decided to write a book over the weekend. I'm going to call it *'Jenny's Dictionary'*. It contains every single word in the English language, spelt correctly of course. Consider this masterpiece my English homework for the rest of the year.

# 10. THE FORWARD PLANNING EXCUSE

I'm getting tired of making up excuses each week for why I forgot my homework . . .

. . . So I decided to spend all night writing a long list of brilliant excuses. Just pick one each week and I'll shrug my shoulders and grin cheekily.

# 11. THE SUPPLY TEACHER EXCUSE

Miss Print, you're not supposed to be teaching your class today. You've got the day off . . .

. . . You've been selected at random to represent the National Teacher Association at *Disney Land's 'Education Day'*. I'll be taking your class, now run along your plane leaves in 20 minutes.

49 Excuses for Not Doing Your Homework

# 12. THE NEW CALENDAR EXCUSE

Haven't you heard, the Government have introduced a brand new Calendar...

| ALL-NEW CALENDAR | | | | | | |
|---|---|---|---|---|---|---|
| SAT1 | SAT2 | SUN1 | SUN2 | MON | SAT3 | SUN3 |
| 28 | 29 | 30 | 31 | 1 | 2 | 3 |
| 4 | 5 | 6 | 7 | 8 | 9 | 10 |
| 11 | 12 | 13 | 14 | 15 | 16 | 17 |
| 18 | 19 | 20 | 21 | 22 | 23 | 24 |
| 25 | 26 | 27 | 28 | 29 | 30 | 1 |

... As you can see we've got a busy week ahead. Plus according to the new calendar today isn't Monday, instead it's Saturday, so I'm going back to bed.

# 13. THE S.B.F. EXCUSE

Timmy's brain has gone on vacation due to S.B.F. Disease (Severe Brain Freeze) . . .

. . . his brain has gone to the Bahamas to thaw off on the beach. Do not set him any homework until his brain has returned (unless the homework is to drool on a piece of paper).

# 14. THE POWERPOINT EXCUSE

I have forgotten my homework, but I have several excellent excuses . . .

. . . please take a seat and I'll show the PowerPoint Presentation I've prepared demonstrating my forgetfulness but positive attitude for the Education System.

# 15. THE HORRIFIC ACCIDENT EXCUSE

I was in a Paper-Round Accident over the summer holiday and broke both my arms . . .

. . . there's a new Super-Computer I could use to do my homework that works through blinking, telepathy and tongue movements. So unless the school can pay for it I can't do any homework for the next 6 months... Did I mention it costs $500,000?

# 16. THE HOMELESS EXCUSE

I couldn't do my homework last night because I no longer have a home . . . I'm homeless . . .

. . . If it was called *'pavement-outside-of-the-local-shop-work'* I would have done it, but it's called *'homework'* so naturally it doesn't apply to me!

# 17. THE ALPHABET EXCUSE

I've realised over the weekend that someone needs to put your teaching skills to question...

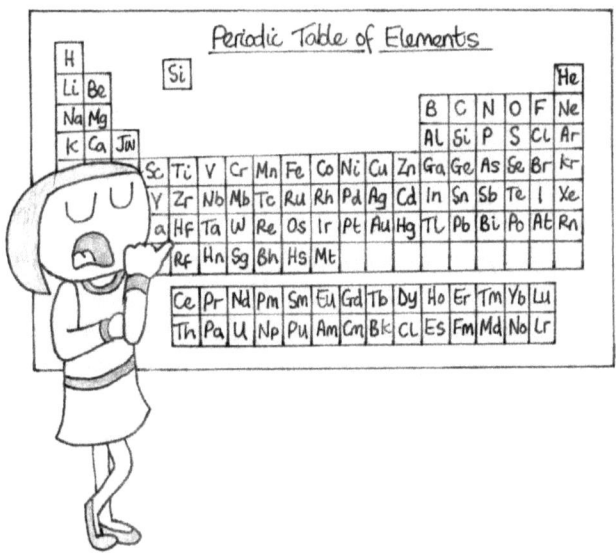

... can we, your class of up-and-coming masterminds, trust you to set our homework when the alphabet poster in your classroom is clearly wrong!

# 18. THE BACK-WORDS EXCUSE

!sdrawkcab kaeps ylno nac I won dna gnorw ylbirroh tnew tnemirepxe ecneics edam-emoh yM . . .

# 19. THE SCIENCE SHOW-DOWN EXCUSE

I told my good friend and mentor that you think you're the best science teacher in the world, so now he has challenged you to a Science-Off . . .

. . . Mr Steven Hawkins said you shouldn't bother setting homework tonight seeing as this pile of books is your revision for the show-down tomorrow. Good luck Miss.

# 20. THE DISEASED EXCUSE

I've got some bad news Miss. I've been diagnosed with Brain & Hand Disease . . .

. . . it's a strain of Foot & Mouth Disease, which means that my brain no longer has control of my arms! They've been wiggling and wobbling like this all weekend. My homework is just one big squiggle.

# 21. THE STUDENT BECOMES THE TEACHER EXCUSE

I believe we, as your students, would learn more if our roles were reversed . . .

. . . and if you don't like what I have to say then sit down and shut up or I will report you to the Headteacher. Now then class, this mornings lesson is a field trip to McDonald's.

# 22. THE HOMEWORK BUDDY EXCUSE

You've never heard of a Homework Buddy . . .

. . . Well Miss, they're like a Pen Pal except instead of simply writing letters you also swap homework. My Homework Buddy, Abu from Peru, is currently doing my homework and I'm doing his. I've got to knit a blanket out of Llama Wool.

# 23. EDUCATION CONSPIRACY EXCUSE

I've been working on a conspiracy theory. We're not in school to colour in, and cut and stick, and play in the playground . . . are we? . . .

. . . you're moulding us into responsible adults that will contribute to our modern society through taking jobs, and paying taxes, and being good citizens. Be warned, I'm on to you!

# 24. THE LOST IT! EXCUSE

Have you heard of the Bermuda Triangle Miss . . .

. . . in the North Atlantic Ocean . . . dangerous waters . . . infamous for paranormal activity . . . Well I accidentally dropped my homework in it on the way to school and a sea monster ate it.

# 25. THE INSANITY EXCUSE

Why did I forget to bring my homework and why am I wearing underpants on my head? . . .

. . . Well Miss, I've recently moved house to the Mental Asylum. This is how my new friends wear underpants. By the way, my doctor says that my new homework is to stop chewing my elbow.

# 26. THE EXTERNAL HELP EXCUSE

Please forward all homework to: derek@domyhomeworkforme.com

# 27. THE 'PRIEST OF THE LAZY WAY' EXCUSE

Now that I have said my Holy Vows I can no longer partake in this worldly activity you call *'homework'*...

... as a *Priest of the Lazy Way* I must set an example to the world by devoting my entire life to doing nothing. Thank you for your support in advance.

# 28. THE MARATHON EXCUSE

My homework is ruined! . . .

. . . I shouldn't have stored my homework in my shoe and then completed a marathon before school.

# 29. THE SHORTCUT EXCUSE

My homework is ruined! . . .

. . . that's the last time I take a shortcut to school through the zoo when the Elephants have got a cold!

# 30. THE LIFT TO SCHOOL EXCUSE

My homework is ruined! . . .

. . . that's the last time I ask my Uncle Roy for a lift. He is a part-time Snake Charmer, part-time Yo-Yo Mechanic, part-time Skydiving Instructor.

# 31. THE SHORTCUT EXCUSE CONT.

My homework is ruined! . . .

. . . that's the last time I take a shortcut to school through the fire swamp.

# 32. THE CLASSIC (WITH A TWIST) EXCUSE

What happened to your homework this week Harry? Did your dog eat it again? . . .

. . . actually my pet goldfish ate my homework, who was eaten by the neighbour's cat, who was eaten by my pet dog. It would be a painstakingly complex surgical procedure to retrieve my homework so let's assume I got all the questions right.

# 33. PSYCHOPATHIC PENCIL CASE EXCUSE

You have got to help me Miss! My pencil case is trying to kill me! . . .

. . . it might look innocent but it's plotting something evil.

# 34. THE STOLEN EXCUSE

Do you know the girl with cute little pigtails, inch thick glasses, always knows the answer to every single question . . .

. . . she stole my homework. You want proof? Just look at the homework. If all the answers are correct then it's definitely mine.

# 35. THE TALENTLESS EXCUSE

I regret to inform you that I cannot do my homework anymore. I am working on my America's Got Talent act . . .

. . . 'The Talentless Kid'. My sister has pushed me around in this cart all summer so that I haven't had to lift a finger. I'm going to become the very first person to become famous for doing absolutely nothing!

# 36. THE HAIRDRESSING EXCUSE

Oh dear! I must have misheard the homework. I thought you said 'don't forget your *comb*work' . . .

. . . this fabulous hair-do took *3* hours of none-stop-combing and three tins of super-strong hairspray.

# 37. THE INACCURATE QUESTION EXCUSE

The Maths question you set yesterday is extremely flawed...

... I went to the train station and took the New York to Washington D.C. train and it took 5 hours and 38 minutes, instead of 2 hours as the question clearly stated. Oh, and you also owe me $85 for the train ticket.

# 38. THE MY PET CALLED... EXCUSE

I didn't forget my homework. Look . . .

. . . this is my adorable pet dog called *Homework*. She needs constant attention, regular walks to the park and a T-Bone Steak every hour. Otherwise she'll become dangerously aggressive and eat all the chairs!

# 39. THE SHORTCUT EXCUSE CONT.

My homework is ruined! . . .

. . . that's the last time I'll take the shortcut over the lake using my homemade jetpack.

# 40. THE LIFT TO SCHOOL EXCUSE CONT.

My homework is ruined! . . .

. . . that's the last time I'll be asking this guy for a lift!

# 41. THE FORGETFUL EXCUSE

I'm sorry Miss, I forgot my homework . . .

. . . you want to hear an excuse? Oh darn it I forgot that too! It took 2 hours to come up with the perfect excuse . . . if only some author would write a book full of brilliant excuses!

# 42. THE SQUARE EYES EXCUSE

I never thought it would happen, but it did. My eyes have gone square! ...

... Here's a note from my Optician explaining that from now on my eyes can only see screens. So until the school buys me an iPad I can't do my homework.

# 43. THE CHARITABLE EXCUSE

I didn't have time to do my homework this weekend because I've been doing charity work non-stop . . .

. . . I cooked and served tomato soup for the homeless in the morning, then I ran the London Marathon as a dolphin, then I wrote a pop song for charity with Bono, and then I helped Mrs. Doris across the road. Quite honestly Miss I think I deserve the morning off!

# 44. THE PRACTISING EXCUSE

What? You didn't say 'don't forget your *gnome*work?' . . .

. . . but I've watched Snow White and the Seven Dwarfs on repeat all weekend. Plus I've learnt all the words to the song 'Hi-Ho, Hi-Ho'.

# 45. THE BIRTHDAY EXCUSE

What . . . your birthday is next month . . .

. . . you mean you're telling me I've been hiding in this present all *weekend* waiting to surprise you, and in doing so missed the homework deadline, when it's not your birthday!

# 46. THE PLAYGROUND ILLNESS EXCUSE

I am terribly sorry to inform you that over the weekend I've become dangerously allergic to . . . *everyone* . . .

. . . When I touch another person they freeze to the spot. I discovered my awful condition when I was playing tag in the playground. Unfortunately I couldn't do my homework because I am the homework for hundreds of scientists while they research a cure.

# 47. THE DEMOTED EXCUSE

Did you not get the memo, you've been demoted to Teaching Assistant...

... Let me introduce you to our new class teacher Mr. Google. We ask a question, you type it and Mr. Google gives us the answer. Simple!

# 48. THE POETRY EXCUSE

I know I forgot my homework again, so instead I wrote you a lovely poem as an apology . . .

. . . and if you are setting English homework this week my poem so counts!

# 49. THE HONEST EXCUSE

Well Miss, in truth I forgot it. Sorry . . .

. . . but I understand why I should do my homework:

1. To improve my intelligence, memory and problem solving skills
2. To keep a positive attitude towards study
3. To learn how to manage my time and work independently
4. To communicate better with my parents
5. To mature into a well-rounded, quick-thinking, high-earning, tax-paying human being.

*[Pause, smile sweetly and engage puppy dog eyes]* So I promise I'll try harder next time and make you, my parents and myself proud.

# BONUS: HAND ILLNESS(ES) EXCUSE

I tried to do my homework but . . .

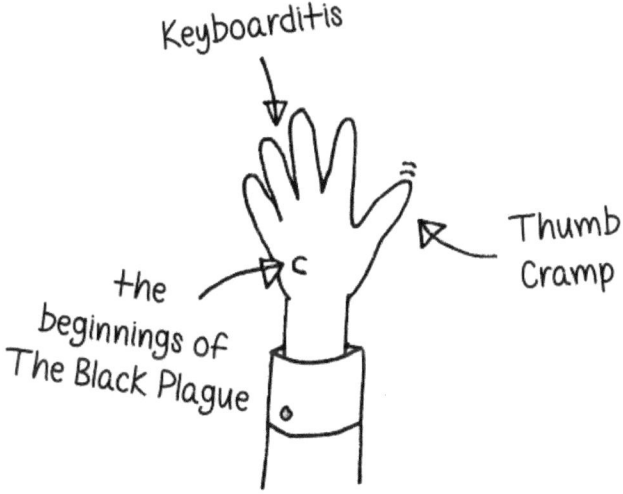

. . . my hand has been struck down by several deadly illnesses.

# BONUS: THESAURUS EXCUSE

I've done my English homework for the rest of my school life...

...I call it the 'Thesaurus'. All the words for all my essays are inside, you'll just have to rearrange them to make the essays yourself.

# BONUS: "I" BEFORE "E" EXCUSE

I'll happily do my English homework
. . .

Weird policies, such as this, are neither scientific or neighbourly and should be reissued to banish the ancient rule forever

. . . once someone has finally sorted out that annoying 'i before e' rule . . . IT DOESN'T WORK!

# BONUS: WHAT DOESN'T KILL YOU EXCUSE

I know I forgot my homework today . . .

. . . but my dad always says 'what doesn't kill you makes you stronger' (and will probably make you write a really really long Facebook post).

# BONUS: COCKY KID EXCUSE

The homework was too easy . . .

. . . However, you've become a much better teacher in my eyes. This is mainly because I've lowered my expectations.

# BONUS: SILLY FACT EXCUSE

Did you know that 70% of women use gas & air during child birth (and 99.9% of men have a cheeky whiff) . . .

. . . What? The homework was not 'bring a silly fact to school'?

# BONUS: AMNESIA EXCUSE

Erm, hi. My doctor says I have amnesia . . .

. . . Are you my teacher? Is this my classroom? What's homework?

# BONUS: BRAIN SURGERY EXCUSE

Don't worry, Sir. I've had experimental brain surgery...

...There's no point in training this one as I've now got Albert Einstein's.

# BONUS: ESSAY EXCUSE

Would you like to read my essay . . .

. . . great, but first you will need to write it and then you can enjoy reading it.

# BONUS: HEAVEN COLLEGE EXCUSE

This is my last day at this deadbeat school...

... I'll be going to a new school that doesn't believe in homework. It's called Heaven College. That's right, I've got a scholarship to become an angel.

# BONUS: SCHOOL/LIFE BALANCE EXCUSE

School is for work and home is for play . . .

School　　　　　　　　Home

. . . END OF DISCUSSION!

# BONUS: SATURDAY PART-ONE EXCUSE

You've can't set any homework today, Sir . . .

. . . Why? Because today isn't Friday, I've renamed it Saturday Part-One. I no longer believe that 'Fridays' exist. So, I need you to respect my beliefs by sending me home so I can start the weekend.

# BONUS: TIGER EXCUSE

A tiger ate my homework . . .

. . . You know, the one who came for tea.

James Warwood is a writer and illustrator who lives on the borders of North Wales with his wife, two sons, and cactus (called Steve the Cactus).

He has a degree in Theology, which at the time seemed like a great idea, until he released he didn't want to become an RE Teacher. Instead, he writes laugh-out-loud middle grade fiction and non-fiction. He also fills them with his silly cartoons. He is the bestselling author of the EXCUSE ENCYCLOPEDIA and the TRUTH OR POOP SERIES.

James likes whiskey, squirrels, reading silly books, playing his bass guitar, and Greggs Sausage Rolls. He does not like losing at board games or having to writing about himself in the third person.

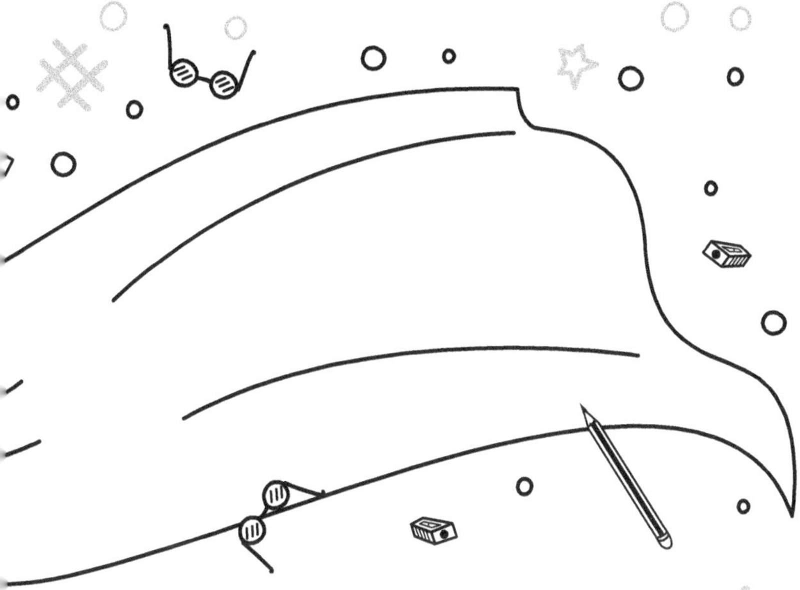

# WHERE TO FIND JAMES ONLINE

Website: www.cjwarwood.com
Goodreads: James Warwood
Instagram: CJWarwood
Facebook: James Warwood

Want to join the
BOOKS & BISCUITS
CLUB?

Scan me to sign up
to the newsletter.

# MIDDLE-GRADE STAND-ALONE FICTION

The Chef Who Cooked Up a Catastrophe
The Boy Who Stole One Million Socks
The Girl Who Vanquished the Dragon

# TRUTH OR POOP SERIES

True or false quiz books.
Learn something new and laugh as you do it!

# THE EXCUSE ENCYCLOPEDIA

11 more books to read!

# GET THEM ALL IN THIS 12 IN 1 BUMPER EDITION!

*820-page compendium of knowledge with 180 BONUS excuses*

Scan me to activate your

## 25% DISCOUNT

www.ingramcontent.com/pod-product-compliance
Lightning Source LLC
Chambersburg PA
CBHW041314110526
44591CB00022B/2908